I0814016

SPACE OBJECTS

THE MOON

by Elizabeth Andrews

Cody Koala
An Imprint of Pop!
popbooksonline.com

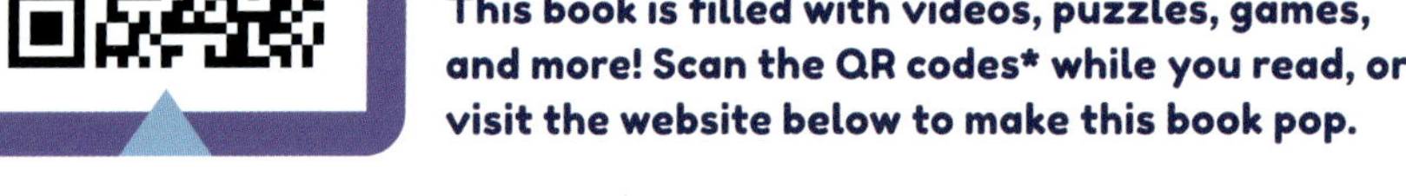

This book is filled with videos, puzzles, games, and more! Scan the QR codes* while you read, or visit the website below to make this book pop.

popbooksonline.com/moon

*Scanning QR codes requires a web-enabled smart device with a QR code reader app and a camera.

abdobooks.com

Published by Pop!, a division of ABDO, PO Box 398166, Minneapolis, Minnesota 55439.

Printed in the United States of America, North Mankato, Minnesota.

102024
012025

THIS BOOK CONTAINS RECYCLED MATERIALS

Cover Photo: NASA
Interior Photos: Getty Images, NASA, Shutterstock Images
Editor: Grace Hansen
Series Designer: Victoria Bates

Library of Congress Control Number: 2024938610

Publisher's Cataloging-in-Publication Data
Names: Andrews, Elizabeth, author.
Title: The moon / by Elizabeth Andrews
Description: Minneapolis, Minnesota : Pop!, 2025 | Series: Space objects | Includes online resources and index
Identifiers: ISBN 9781098246976 (lib. bdg.) | ISBN 9781098247539 (ebook)
Subjects: LCSH: Outer space--Exploration--Juvenile literature. | Moon--Juvenile literature. | Solar system—Juvenile literature. | Astronomy--Juvenile literature. | Satellites--Juvenile literature. | Universe--Juvenile literature.
Classification: DDC 523.3--dc23

Table of Contents

Chapter 1

How the Moon Formed

More than 4.5 billion years ago, **gravity** combined gas and dust to create our **solar system**. It includes the Sun, eight planets, and thousands of other smaller objects such as moons.

Watch a video here!

Earth's only moon is 4.53 billion years old. It is the second-brightest body

The moon sits 238,855 miles (384,400km) away from Earth.

in our sky. The moon does not shine by itself. It reflects sunlight off its surface.

Some scientists believe the moon formed after a smaller planet hit Earth. The planet broke apart along with pieces of Earth. Gravity brought those pieces together to form the moon. It was pulled into Earth's **orbit**.

Other planets in the solar system have their own moons.

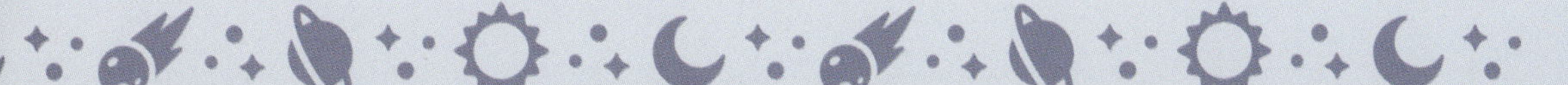

Chapter 2

Moon Materials

The moon has different layers. It has an iron core, mantle, and crust. The moon was once covered in a sea of **magma**. As the magma cooled, it formed the moon's hard surface.

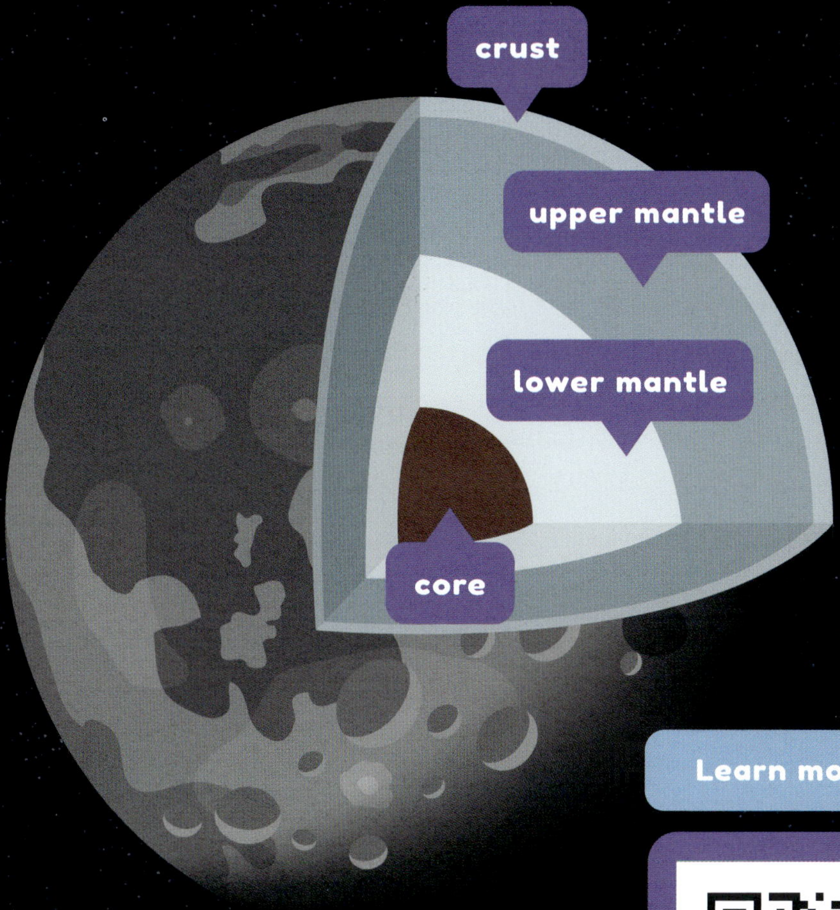

crust

upper mantle

lower mantle

core

Learn more here!

Some other materials that make up the moon are oxygen, magnesium, and silicon.

The moon has dark and light spots. These are craters with high and low ground.

Some people think the craters make the moon look like it is made of cheese.

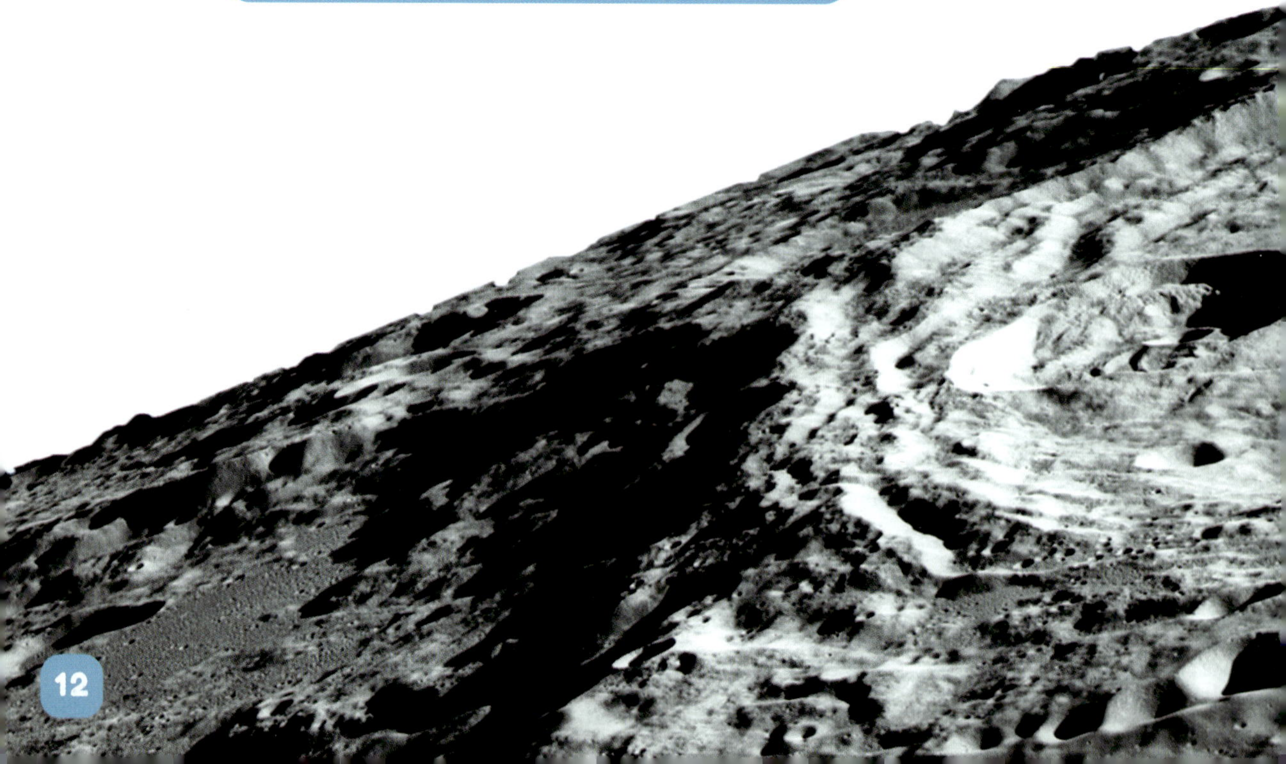

Many of the craters were created when **asteroids** and **comets** hit the moon.

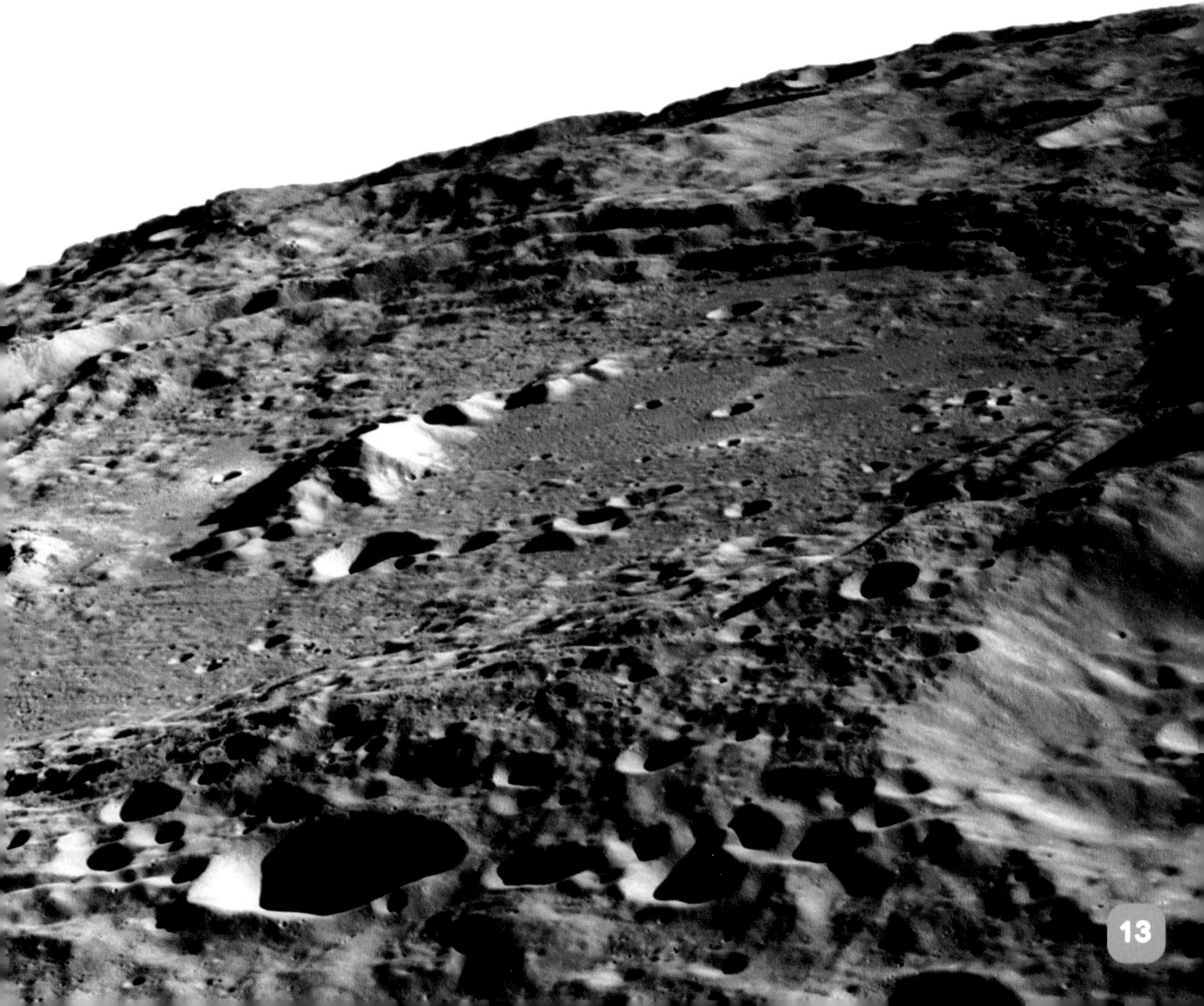

Chapter 3

Moon Movements

The Earth and the moon are always moving. The Earth spins on its **axis** while it **orbits** the Sun. The moon orbits the Earth. These movements create the moon's phases.

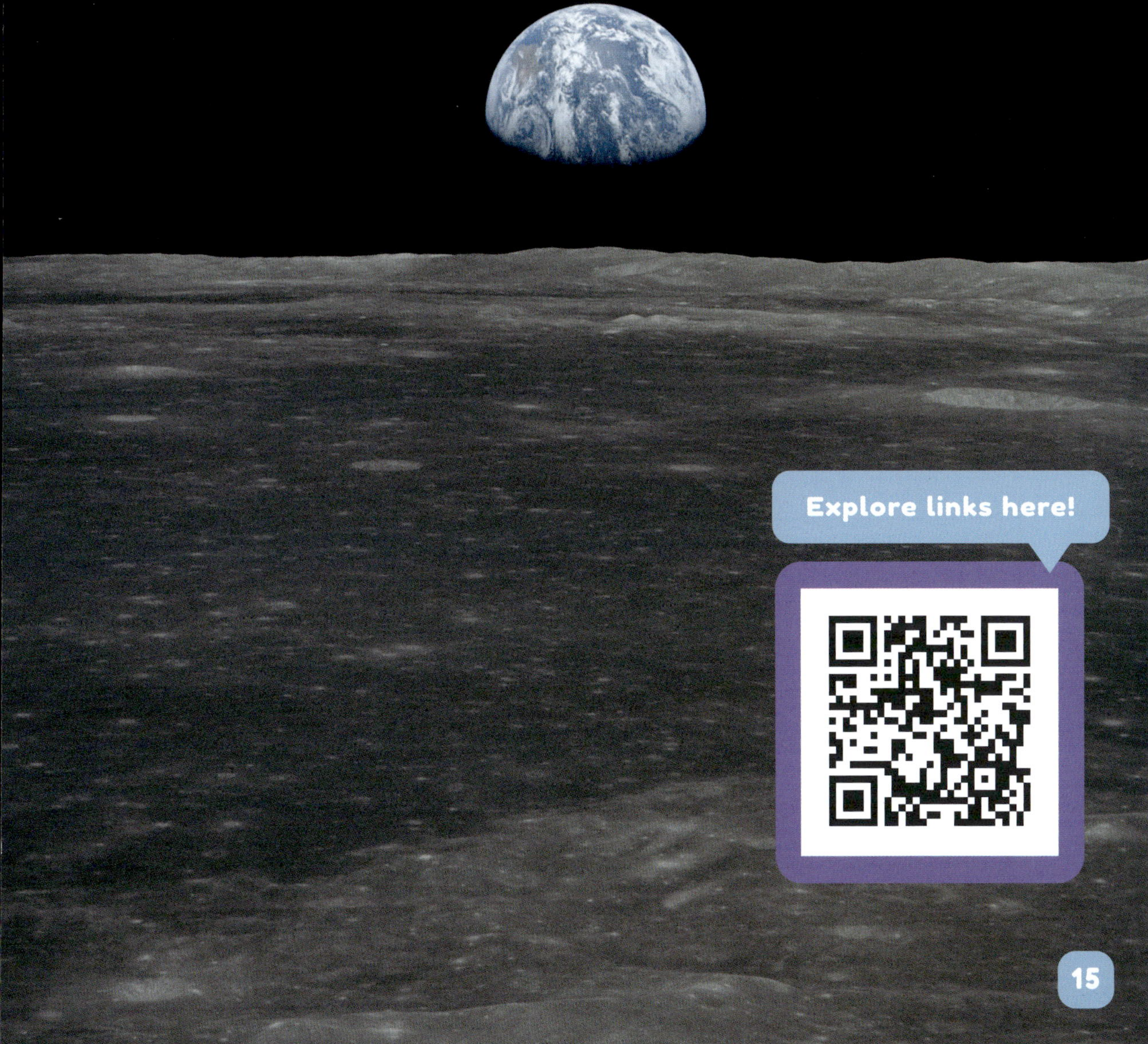
Explore links here!

The moon is called a new moon at the beginning of its orbit. The moon sits between the Sun and Earth. Sunlight hits the side of the moon that isn't visible from Earth.

Two weeks later, the moon is full and bright. The Earth sits between the Sun and moon. The Sun's light shines on the side of the moon we can see.

The moon takes 29.5 days to go through all of its phases.

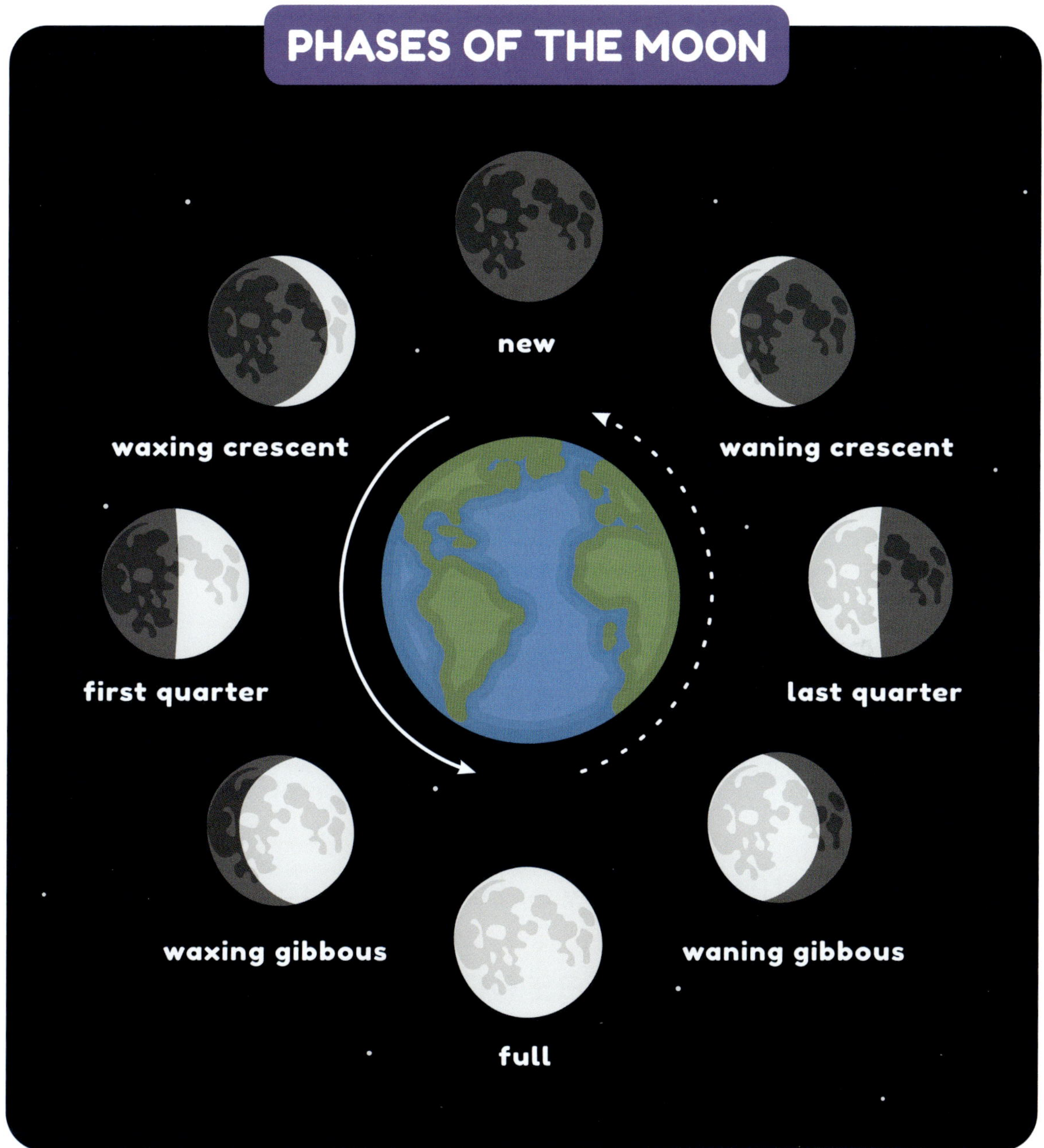
PHASES OF THE MOON
new
waxing crescent
waning crescent
first quarter
last quarter
waxing gibbous
waning gibbous
full

Chapter 4

The Moon's Gravity

The moon has its own **gravity**. It is not as strong as Earth's. But it is strong enough to keep rocks and astronauts from floating away. The moon's gravity creates ocean tides by pulling water toward it.

Complete an activity here!

Making Connections

Text-to-Self

Which phase of the moon is your favorite?

Text-to-Text

Have you read any books about other space objects? If so, how were those objects similar to or different from the moon?

Text-to-World

In the 1950s and 1960s, two countries were trying to send the first humans to the moon. With the help of an adult, research the countries and learn which one made it to the moon first. Write a few sentences about what you learned.

Glossary

asteroid – a small rocky body that orbits the Sun.

axis – an imaginary line through a space object, around which the object turns.

comet – a space object made of ice and dust with a tail of gas.

gravity – a force that pulls objects toward each other.

magma – extremely hot liquid rock.

orbit – the path of a space object as it moves around another space object. To orbit is to follow this path.

solar system – a group of planets and other space objects that revolve around the Sun and are held together by the Sun's gravity.

Index

Online Resources

popbooksonline.com

Thanks for reading this Cody Koala book!

This book is filled with videos, puzzles, games, and more! Scan the QR codes* while you read, or visit the website below to make this book pop.

popbooksonline.com/moon

*Scanning QR codes requires a web-enabled smart device with a QR code reader app and a camera.